Gone Forever!
Triceratops

Rupert Matthews

Heinemann Library
Chicago, Illinois

Designed by Ron Kamen and Paul Davies & Associates
Illustrations by Maureen and Gordon Gray, James Field (SGA), and Darren Lingard
Originated by Ambassador Litho Ltd.
Printed and bound in China by South China Printing Company

07 06 05 04 03
10 9 8 7 6 5 4 3 2 1

Library of Congress Cataloging-in-Publication Data
Matthews, Rupert.
  Triceratops / Rupert Matthews.
      p. cm. -- (Gone forever)
Includes index.
Summary: Describes what has been learned about the physical features,
behavior, and surroundings of the long-extinct triceratops.
  ISBN 1-40340-792-4 (HC), 1-4034-3421-2 (Pbk)
  1. Triceratops--Juvenile literature. [1. Triceratops. 2. Dinosaurs.]
I. Title. II. Gone forever (Heinemann Library)
  QE862.O65 M37 2003
  567.915'8--dc21
                         2002003753

Acknowledgments
The author and publishers are grateful to the following for permission to reproduce copyright material:
p. 4 Libby Montana/Geoscience Books; p. 6 Science Photo Library; pp. 8, 10, 14, 20 Natural History Museum, London;
pp. 12, 18, 24 Francois Gohier/Ardea; p. 16 Ken Lucas/Visuals Unlimited; p. 22 Danny Lehman/Corbis; p. 26 Royal Tyrell Museum, Canada.
Cover photograph reproduced with permission of Francois Gohier/Ardea.

Every effort has been made to contact copyright holders of any material reproduced in this book. Any omissions will be rectified in subsequent printings if notice is given to the publisher.
Special thanks to Dr. Peter Mackovicky for his review of this book.

Some words are shown in bold, **like this.** You can find out what they mean by looking in the glossary.

Contents

Gone Forever!

Many different types of animals lived millions of years ago. Today, most of these animals are **extinct.** This means that they have all died. We find out about them by studying their **fossils.**

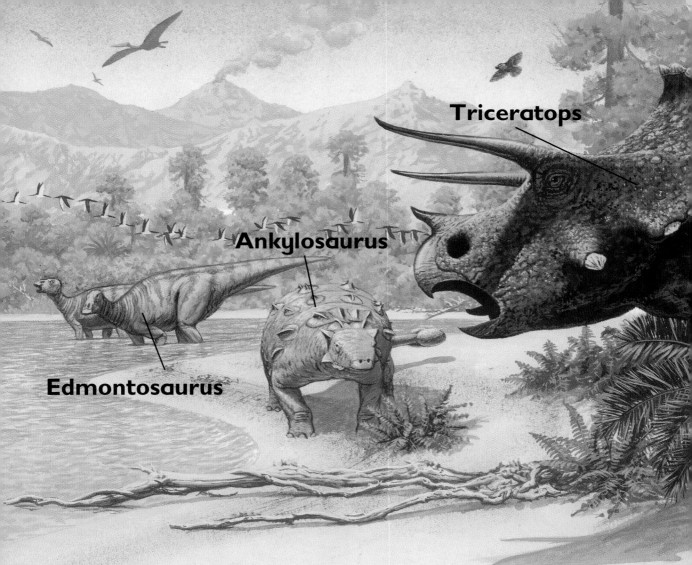

Triceratops

Ankylosaurus

Edmontosaurus

Triceratops was an animal that is now extinct. This type of **dinosaur** lived in North America about 65 million years ago. Many other animals lived at the same time as Triceratops.

5

Triceratops' Home

Scientists study rocks that have Triceratops **fossils** in them. They learn from the rocks what the land was like when Triceratops lived. They learn what the weather was like, too.

Triceratops lived in a land of hills. There were tall mountains and **volcanoes** close by. Wide rivers ran through the hills. The weather was warm and it rained often.

Plants

Plants can become trapped in the ground. After millions of years, they become **fossils.** These fossils can tell us what sorts of plants lived when Triceratops was alive. Many kinds of plants grew at this time.

fossil of a leaf

Triceratops ate bushes and other plants.
There were a lot of short bushes at the time
of Triceratops. This meant there was enough
food for many Triceratops.

Sharing the Food

Other **dinosaurs** lived at the same time as Triceratops. The **fossils** of these dinosaurs tell us how they lived. **Hadrosaurs** were dinosaurs that ate plants, too, just like Triceratops.

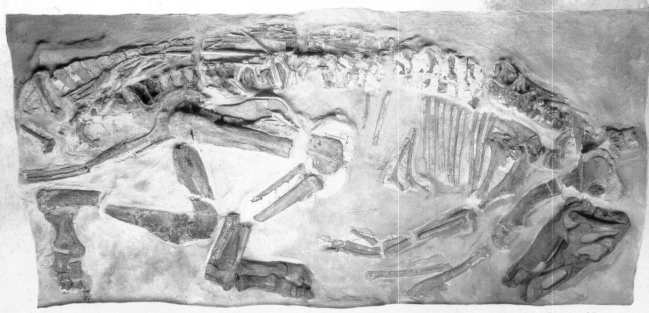

hadrosaur fossils

Hadrosaurs grew to be as long as a school bus. They had teeth that could chew tough leaves. Hadrosaurs ate pine needles and the leaves of other **fir trees.** They could share the land with Triceratops because they ate different kinds of plants.

What Was Triceratops?

Fossil bones of Triceratops have been found and put together. They can be seen in museums. The bones tell us what Triceratops looked like and how it lived.

Triceratops was a large **dinosaur**. It had two
long horns and one short horn on its **skull**.
There was a large **frill** of bone growing from the
back of its head. The name Triceratops means
three-horn-face.

In the Nest

Oviraptor eggs

Dinosaur eggs have been found as **fossils.**
Some of these are still in the nests where they
were laid. They show that dinosaurs built nests
and laid eggs. The Oviraptor eggs shown on
this page are 90 million years old.

Scientists do not know what Triceratops nests looked like. A mother Triceratops may have dug a round hole in the ground. Then, she may have laid her eggs inside the hole. Finally, she may have put a pile of leaves over the eggs to protect them.

Growing Up

Fossils of young Triceratops have not been found. But scientists think their horns were short. However, even a baby Triceratops had a long bone **frill.** This Triceratops was almost an adult. The horns of a baby Triceratops would probably have been much shorter.

16

Young Triceratops probably stayed close to their mother. They learned what plants were good to eat by watching their mother. A mother also guarded her young from meat-eating **dinosaurs.**

17

On the Move

The **fossil** bones of Triceratops' legs tell us how it moved. The legs are made of thick bones. They had to be strong to support the heavy body. The bones also show that there were very strong muscles on all four legs.

leg bones

toes

18

Triceratops walked slowly most of the time.
It moved from bush to bush to find food. But
Triceratops could run fast, too. When it ran,
the heavy Triceratops would have been very
hard to stop!

A Big Bite

The **fossil skull** of Triceratops shows us how it ate. The **beak** was used to nip off leaves and twigs. The strong teeth then chewed the leaves. The cheeks stopped the food from falling out while it was being chewed.

frill

beak

teeth

20

Triceratops had powerful jaw muscles and long rows of teeth. It could chew food into small pieces before it was swallowed. Triceratops had one of the most powerful bites of all the **dinosaurs.**

Living in a Herd

Fossil footprints from **dinosaurs** like Triceratops have been found together. These show that Triceratops probably lived in **herds.** The footprints also show us that dinosaurs of different ages lived together.

Triceratops herds often spread out to look for food. But the herd would form a tight group in times of danger. The largest animals would guard the smaller, weaker animals.

23

Danger!

Scientists have found teeth marks on **fossil** bones of Triceratops. The teeth marks usually belong to the **Tyrannosaurus rex dinosaur.** It had powerful jaws and very sharp teeth.

Tyrannosaurus rex jaws

A Triceratops could sometimes fight off Tyrannosaurus rex. It would point its horns and charge. The horns could hurt Tyrannosaurus rex very badly.

Leading the Herd

The **skulls** of some Triceratops show marks made by the horns of other Triceratops. This shows us that they sometimes fought each other. Perhaps they battled to decide who would lead the **herd.**

Sometimes one Triceratops would try to scare off
another by waving its **frill.** If neither animal backed
away, a fight would begin. They would lock horns
and push against each other. Finally, one
Triceratops would give in. The fight would stop.

Where Did Triceratops Live?

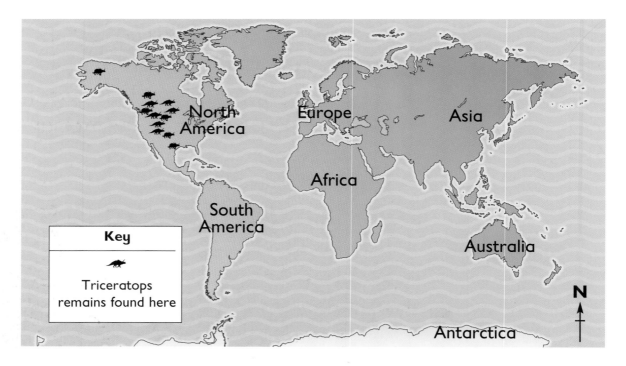

Key

Triceratops remains found here

Triceratops lived in what is now North America. It lived where it could find bushes to eat. Other **dinosaurs** that were like Triceratops lived in other parts of North America.

When Did Triceratops Live?

Triceratops was one of the last **dinosaurs.** It lived right up to the end of the Age of Dinosaurs. Triceratops became **extinct** about 65 million years ago. All other types of dinosaurs became extinct at the same time.

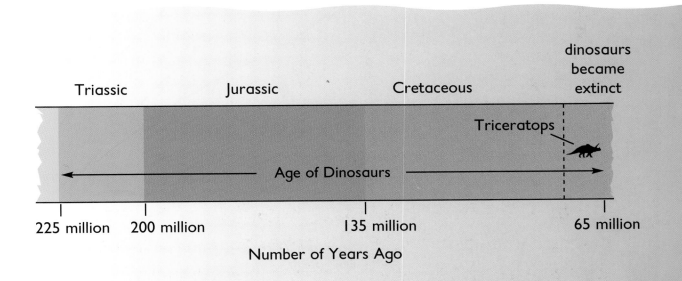

Triassic   Jurassic   Cretaceous   dinosaurs became extinct

Age of Dinosaurs

Triceratops

225 million   200 million   135 million   65 million

Number of Years Ago

29

Fact File

Triceratops	
Length:	30 feet (9 meters)
Height:	16 feet, 5 inches (5 meters)
Weight:	6 and a half tons (6 metric tons)
Time:	Late Cretaceous Period, about 65 million years ago
Place:	North America

How to Say It

dinosaur—dine-ah-sor

Hadrosaur—had-rah-sor

Triceratops—try-ser-ah-tops

Tyrannosaurus—teh-ran-ah-sor-us

Glossary

beak hard, pointed tip at the front of the mouth

dinosaur one of a large group of extinct reptiles that lived on Earth millions of years ago.

extinct no longer living on Earth

fir tree tree that keeps its leaves all year. The leaves are skinny and always green.

fossil remains of a plant or animal, usually found inside rocks. Most fossils are from hard parts like bones and teeth. Some fossils are traces of animals, such as their footprints.

frill bone at the back of Triceratops' head

Hadrosaur large plant-eating dinosaur that lived at the same time as Triceratops

herd large group of plant-eating animals that live together

skull the bones of the head

Tyrannosaurus rex large meat-eating dinosaur. Tyrannosaurus rex hunted Triceratops, Hadrosaurs and other plant-eating dinosaurs.

volcano opening in the earth's surface where hot rocks, lava and ash come out

More Books to Read

Cohen, Daniel. *Triceratops*. Mankato, Minn.: Capstone Press, 2000.

Gaines, Richard. *Triceratops*. Edina, Minn.: Abdo Publishing Company, 2001.

Olshevsky, George and Sandy Fritz. *Triceratops*. Mankato, Minn.: Smart Apple Media, 2002.

Index